...and the shepherd Bénezet built a bridge for AVIGNON

Texts by Renée Lefranc
Director, Educational Department,
Assistant Curator,
under the Direction of Dominique Vingtain,
Curator, Palace of the Popes
Translated from the French by Mary Podevin

EDITIONS RMG

SAINT BÉNEZET,
MINGLING HISTORY AND LEGEND

The Pont d'Avignon is one of the best-known monuments in the world, and this is partly because of the beloved children's song, familiar throughout the entire world - even in China, where they say it is taught at school! However, although the bridge might be famous, its actual history is much less well known and understood. When people see it for the first time, they are often surprised to see that it is broken. Only four arches remain standing ! What happened to all the others ? How did they disappear ? What happened to cause the destruction of the bridge ? And what about the name of the bridge - do you know the real name of the "Pont d'Avignon" ? The bridge is actually called the Saint Bénezet bridge - which makes one wonder just who Saint Bénezet was, and why the bridge was named after him. In reading about the history of the bridge, you will be taken back in time to an era of legends, when many stories began with the words "once upon a time", opening the door onto dreams. Yet, the most beautiful legends are often based on real facts, and they help us learn and remember past history.

So let us begin, back in the year of Grace 1177, when there was child named Benoît who built a bridge in Avignon, thanks to miraculous assistance from Jesus Christ ....

Bénezet is the Provençal version of the name **Benoît**.

THE LEGEND

The legend starts with young **Benoît**, a simple shepherd, as he sat watching his mother's flock of sheep grazing in the meadow, on a day when an eclipse of the sun occurred. As he sat tending the sheep, he heard a loud voice which said:

"Benoît, my son, listen to the voice of Jesus Christ."

"Who are you, my Lord, that you are speaking to me ? I hear your voice, but I cannot see you".

"Listen to me, Benoît, and do not be afraid. I am Jesus Christ who with a single word created the heavens, the earth, the seas and all the life they contain".

"Lord, what do you want me to do ?", replied Benoît.

"I want you to leave your mother's sheep that you are watching over, for you must build me a bridge over the Rhone", said the voice of the Lord.

"Lord, I do not know the Rhone and I dare not abandon my mother's sheep", answered Benoît.

"Have I not told you to follow my word ? Come then bravely, I will take care of the sheep and I will give you a companion to take you all the way to the Rhone."

"But my Lord", protested Benoît, "I have only three coins; how can I build a bridge over the Rhone ?"

"You will build it very well, doing just as I tell you."

Benoît obeyed the voice, and started down the road. Just as he was walking, an angel appeared on his path. The angel had taken on the appearance of a pilgrim traveler, walking with a stick and a bag slung over his shoulder. The traveler said to Benezet:

"Follow me and do not fear, for I will lead you to the place where you are to build a bridge for Jesus Christ, and I will show you how to build it."

An **"obole"** or obolus is an old French coin which was worth half of one **denier**, which was like a penny. It took 240 deniers to make one pound. Bénezet therefore paid one half of the sum that the ferryman had demanded.

Avignon

Le Rhône

As they neared the river, Benoît, who was really quite frightened, declared that he could never build a bridge that was long enough to cross the river. The angel replied:

"Do not fear, for the Holy Spirit is with you. Do you see that little boat ? You must use it to cross the river. Go to the city of Avignon, go and see the Bishop and his people."

And the angel vanished.

Benoît drew closer to the ferrymen and asked them to ferry him over to the other bank, all the way to the city, "for the love of God and the Blessed Virgin". The owner of the boat, who was Jewish, retorted:

"If you want to cross the river, you must give me three **deniers**, like anybody else."

Benoît once again invoked the love of God and the Virgin Mary, and begged the Jewish ferryman to let him cross, but the ferryman replied:

"I care nothing about your Mary, she has no power over heaven or earth. I much prefer three pennies than the love of Mary; there's no lack of Marys around here."

Benoît gave him the three **oboles**, or coins, that he had - the only money that he possessed. Realizing that was all he would ever get, the Jew took them and ferried Benoît across the river. Benoît went straight to find the **Bishop** who was preaching to his congregation, and spoke up loudly:

"Listen to me and know that Jesus Christ has sent me to you to build a bridge over the Rhone."

Upon seeing the young boy, the Bishop sent him straight to the **prévôt** or **viguier**, who was the Provost of the city, "to skin him alive and cut off his hands and feet, for he could be nothing other than a very bad man and a dangerous gladiator".

Benoît, who remained unmoved by such words, repeated his message
once again:
"Monsignor, Jesus Christ has sent me to this city for the purpose of
building a bridge over the Rhone".
The Provost said:
"Just how, vile young thing who owns nothing, can you brag that
you are going to build a bridge where no one, not even God, nor
Peter, nor Paul, not even Charlemagne, nor anyone else, has ever
been able to do such a thing ? Is this not totally outrageous ?
However, since everyone knows that bridges are built with stones
and mortar, I will give you a stone that I have in my **palace**, and if
you can move it and carry it, I will believe that you are indeed
capable of building a bridge".
Benoît, placing all his trust in God, went back to the Bishop and told him
that he would succeed in accomplishing the task set by the Provost.
"Then", said the Bishop, "let us go and behold the marvels that you
promise to accomplish".
The Bishop and the entire population thus attended the miracle which
then followed. Benoît, facing a huge stone that thirty men could never
have budged, lifted the stone with astonishing ease and carried it to the
place which was to become the base of the first arch of the bridge.
The crowd, overwhelmed at what they had seen, understood that this was
a miracle, and the Provost immediately called Benoît a saint and kissed
his hands and feet, offering him three hundred sous. That very day,
Benoît collected five thousand sous and accomplished eighteen other
miracles ! He healed the blind, the deaf and the crippled by laying a cross
upon them and saying "May your faith heal you".

In the south of France, the **viguier**, or provost, is a magistrate who acted as the head of the police in the city. At Bénezet's time, the provost performed his duties at the **palais de la Commune**, or Town Palace.

In the early 12th century, elected magistrates, who were consuls or podestas, governed Avignon, presided over by the bishop. This group of lords, called the **Commune,** lived in a castle located on the Rocher des Doms, which had previously been home to a count. The castle was near the Bishop's palace, and slightly below it, on the southern slope, the Commune also had a palace from which they governed. One of the palace walls can still be seen above the rue de la Peyrolerie. In 1834, a large stone tympanum, portraying a knight, was found in the courtyard. This tympanum most certainly embellished the doorway to this palace.

Peyrolerie Street

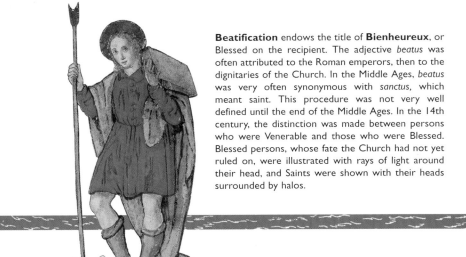

Beatification endows the title of **Bienheureux**, or Blessed on the recipient. The adjective *beatus* was often attributed to the Roman emperors, then to the dignitaries of the Church. In the Middle Ages, *beatus* was very often synonymous with *sanctus,* which meant saint. This procedure was not very well defined until the end of the Middle Ages. In the 14th century, the distinction was made between persons who were Venerable and those who were Blessed. Blessed persons, whose fate the Church had not yet ruled on, were illustrated with rays of light around their head, and Saints were shown with their heads surrounded by halos.

This marvelous tale most certainly reminds you of other stories that you have read or heard. Like many other remarkable persons, Benoît began his adventure marked by a sign from above - in this case, the eclipse of the sun that occurred while he was guarding his mother's sheep. The planets, positioned in an unusual order, are a sign that extraordinary events are about to unfold. Like Joan of Arc, Bénezet was of very humble origins. He was a simple child, with no money and no education. But God always chooses pure and innocent beings to accomplish his intentions. The hero then usually faces countless obstacles before fulfilling his mission. Benezet went through a series of initiation rites, overcoming adversity, braving the mockery and even rejection by his fellow man. In the end, just like King Arthur who had to pull the sword Excalibur from the rock in which it was plunged, something no one else had ever been able to do, the young shepherd had to lift a massive stone. This feat, which of course was beyond his normal ability, suggested divine intervention, which in this case meant sainthood for Bénezet, just as it meant royal majesty for Arthur.

The story of Benoît's miraculous lifting of the stone was written down on a parchment which is still preserved at the Vaucluse Departmental Archives. The story was written in Latin, and was translated in 1889 by A.B. de Saint-Venant, an engineer and a member of the Institute, in his text "Saint Bénezet, Patron Saint of Engineers". The parchment tells the story not only of the saint's life, but it also described the **miracles** which occurred on his tomb. Historians have dated the parchment at the end of the 13th century.

During the Middle Ages, such legendary texts were used by alms collectors, who traveled throughout the area to collect money. This type of story was read from the pulpit, or posted on the doors of the churches, to rouse the faithful and incite them to be generous and make a donation on behalf of a specific mission, in this case the bridge. In exchange, anyone who gave alms obtained an **indulgence** from the Pope, which meant that the donor's sins were forgiven. This was a purely materialistic way to redeem one's sins. The first indulgence granted for the donations made for the bridge was bestowed by Pope Innocent III, on the 3rd of September 1209. The sums of money which were raised were used to repair and maintain the bridge. In the 15th century, such alms-collecting tactics were widespread throughout all of Europe !

Indulgence means the remission of temporal punishment due for a sin after the guilt has been forgiven. The Pope or the Bishops judge the conditions in which they will grant pardon and allow indulgence, in exchange for pious acts, which could consist of prayer or mortification (fasting, pilgrimage, wearing a hair shirt ...) As of the 6th century, influenced by the barbarian tribes who exacted a price for every fault committed, the Church published books which listed the various prices of penitence. By the 9th century, this system had become corrupted, and every fault was automatically expressed in terms of a sum of money, set by the clergy. The clergy was naturally often tempted to serve its own interests when setting the price for the redemption of sins.

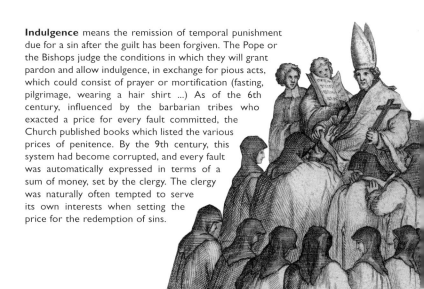

The **Porte Ferruce** (porta *Ferrussa*), or Ferruce entrance into the ramparts, was located between the butcher shop and the Albano House, now the Town Hall. The street running from the Ferruce Gate was also called "Mirailherie" street (which meant Street of Mirrors) and led to the Palace. Nowadays, Ferruce street leads to the Pont d'Avignon.

THE MIRACLES

This tale, told on the parchment which is preserved at the Vaucluse Departmental Archives, is followed by testimony from witnesses, which leaves room to think that a **canonization process** had been started, though today there remains no such trace. The declarations which are reported on the parchment were made twenty years after Bénezet's death. They confirm that the young man did indeed lift the first stone of the bridge which was then built over a period of seven years. They also tell about several miracles which occurred both before and after Bénezet's death. Here a few examples of the miracles which were described on the parchment.

When the workers ran out of stones to build the bridge, the saint pointed to spots where they would dig and find stones. A blind woman, whose eyesight he had restored, would lose her sight again every time she would move away from the bridge. She therefore entered into the service of the Bridge Works (an order of laypersons who cared for the travelers) for one year and definitively recovered her eyesight. One night, in a church in Burgundy, the devil threw a stone at Bénézet while he was praying, trying to kill him, but he missed. Wild with rage at his own clumsiness, the devil then went to the Pont

A **miracle** (from the Latin *miraculum*: wonder) is an extraordinary event which is held to be an act of God.

d'Avignon, and destroyed one of the bridge piers. Through divination, Bénézet knew what had happened. He told his companions to return to Avignon to repair the bridge.Other witnesses had visions of the completed bridge when construction had only just begun.

One day, on the square just in front of the **porte Ferruce**, a man was gambling and taking the name of the Lord in vain. Benoît, who just happened to be passing by, heard the man and overturned the game with his walking stick. This made the other players very angry. One of them slapped the saint. Just then, the head of the man who had slapped Benoît started swinging round and round on his neck, turning like a screw. A woman said: "May God forgive you". Benoît prayed for his aggressor and his head went back to normal. Benoît resisted drinking wine. Yet, three different times, God changed water into wine for him and his companions. A man who had harvested the fields on Saint Peter's feast day found his hand stuck to the scythe and to the wheat he had cut. He went to pray on Bénézet's grave and was delivered. He left his scythe and the wheat on the tomb.

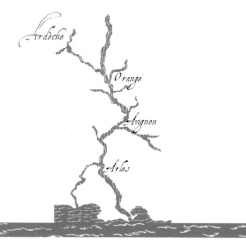

Saint Bénezet's house in Le Villard, town of Burzet in Ardèche

THE HISTORICAL FACTS

All the various tales about Bénezet describe him as an adolescent. When his relics, which we will discuss later, were examined, this was confirmed. There are varying traditions concerning his place of birth, however historians tend to agree that Bénezet was born in Le Villard, a tiny hamlet in Ardèche, near Burzet. There, in Le Villard, a stone topped with a cross marks the point where the young shepherd gazed at his home town for the last time, before going down the road ... His own home is still there. Yet another town, Hermillon, near Saint-Jean-de-Maurienne, also claims to be home to Bénezet. However, the house in Hermillon was destroyed during World War II. Fortunately, however, there is still a rock there, on the hillside, worn away where Bénezet used to kneel in prayer !

The chronicles telling the story of Bénezet are historical texts and not legends. They describe him as **"Bienheureux"**, or blessed. In reading these chronicles, we learn that Bénezet was apparently also responsible for the construction of another bridge, the Guillotière Bridge in Lyon, and that he died in 1184, approximately seven years after beginning the bridge in Avignon, where he was buried.

Bénezet's role in the construction of the bridge was quite significant. He became the **patron** saint of building engineers, not because of his technical prowess, but because he was a true leader of men. Solely through his persuasive powers, he succeeded in rousing an entire population and uniting them behind the bridge, a project that served the public interest. His preaching moved the crowds who gathered to listen to him. In the year 1200, the canon of Laon, a chronicler, described the large assemblies who came to hear Bénezet's sermons, adding that he had never seen such numbers. And yet, when Bénezet spoke, he was quite simple in his manner, and did not possess any special talent as an orator. He was, we are told, without any particular elegance. Despite these observations, he radiated something special, to such an extent that one and all, even the greatest, knelt before him, and tore at his clothing to get a piece for themselves ! A true star ! Bénezet put his charisma to work for the bridge. He quickly started raising the money which enabled him to see his project through. This very feat, which seemed far beyond his abilities, already stood out as a miracle in itself, and was widely acknowledged by his contemporaries.

The **parish** (from the Greek *paroikia*: group of neighboring dwellings) is a territorial division of the city administered to by a priest who belonged to the **parish church**. During the Middle Ages, there were seven parishes in the city of Avignon: Saint Peter, Saint Didier, Notre-Dame-de-la-Principale, Saint Géniès, Saint Symphorien, Saint Stephen and Saint-Agricol. The **parish cemeteries** next to the churches were just about the only open spaces available in the crowded town. They were not walled in and served as public squares, where meetings, fairs and markets were often held, and where official deeds and contracts were signed !

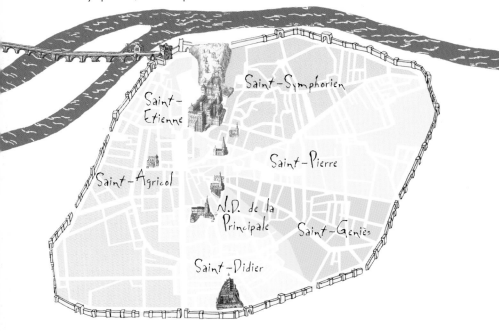

Like a pilgrim, he went from town to town, all the way to the city of Langres, to gather alms, plead for donations, and finance his work. Just next to the bridge, he also built a charitable institution, as was the custom in the Middle Ages, to lodge the travelers and pilgrims who arrived in Avignon at night, when the rampart gates were already closed. Travelers could also get medical care there, if necessary. This building was both a hospice and a hospital, and later, a chapel was added. In 1187, the bishop authorized the creation of a cemetery, which was reserved only for foreigners and the lay brothers, so as not to compete with the **parish cemeteries**. The "Œuvre du Pont", or the Bridge Works, was a group of **laymen** called the Brothers of the Bridge Works, or "Frères de l'œuvre". They lived as a community, but unlike monks, they had taken no vows. They were called *fratres donati*, the Donatus brothers, for they devoted themselves to the Work, in a spirit of charity, inspired by Bénezet who was their leader.

A **layperson** is someone who is not a member of the clergy.

MOT FAVET.

✝ IESVS MARIA
✝ IOSEPH.

GRIFFES.

Sainct Benezet
Fundateur du pont
S D'Auignon.

The **canonization** of a saint (from the Greek *kanôn*: the rule) is an essential right which is reserved for the Pope. Canonization sets a man of God apart from ordinary mankind as a model of virtue. The idea of sainthood has evolved over time, taking on increasingly specific and limited meaning. Sainthood is officially recognized by the a solemn liturgy on the anniversary of the death of the saint, or if the date of the death is not known, on the day of the translation of the saint's relics. The verb *canonizare* appeared in the early 11th century. Doubts had been expressed concerning the authenticity of some of the martyrs. After examining each case, the Bishops had to pronounce a judgment, and authorize public worship. Their texts then traveled from one diocese to the next. To make these judgments, the criteria for veritable sainthood had to be defined. Charlemagne and Louis the Pious ruled on the matter, and it was forbidden to venerate saints who were not authorized. Investigations were held into candidates for sainthood, and in the 11th and 12th centuries, the papacy reserved the right to make the final ruling on such investigations.

17

In church liturgy, the **Proper** is the part of the celebration which relates to a saint, a time or a place which is not part of the **Ordinary**, which means the set of unchanging prayers, or the **Common**, which is the office that the Roman Catholic Church has defined for all cases.

Martyrology is a list of the martyrs who have suffered and died because of their belief in God. The martyrs were the first saints worshipped by the Christians, both in the Roman Empire and in the Orient. To keep up the cult of these saints, the bishops exhorted the faithful to list their saints in a martyrology. In the 4th century, documents recorded their lives and the circumstances of their deaths. These *Acta* or *Vitae* constituted proof of their sainthood and also provided a way to spread their reputation.

Apparently, Bénezet was not canonized. However, Pope John XXII officially recognized his sainthood, in making the bridge priory and chapel part of the parish of the Saint Agricol **Collegiate Church**, where religious services took place. In 1331, the pope had a religious service composed for Saint Bénezet and included it in the **Proper** of Saint Agricol. The feast day of Saint Benoît of the bridge, Confessor, was set on April 14th. During the celebration of this special service, the priest recalled the fact that the popes had granted indulgences to the faithful who visited his chapel, and called to mind the saint's miracles, which he had performed primarily for the deaf, the blind and the lame. In the 16th century, Bénezet was added to the **martyrology** and in the 17th century, his special service was printed. He then become one of the **patron saints of Avignon**. Devotion to Saint Bénezet was quite fervent. The great esteem in which he was held is clearly reflected in the large number of works of art which illustrate his legend.

A **collegiate church** has a chapter (or assembly) of canons who live in community according to a rule.

Saint-Agricol

The patron saints of Avignon

The **patron saint** (from the Latin *patronus*: protector) is the saint whose protection is implored by the cities, the brotherhoods, the guilds... In addition to Bénezet, the city of Avignon also has several other patron saints, such as Saint Martha, Saint Agricol, Saint Ruf, Pierre de Luxembourg, and many others.

Pierre de Luxembourg, born in Lorraine in 1369, was on speaking terms with all the European rulers. Orphaned at a very early age, he was sent to Paris to study. At the age of 8 he made a vow of chastity, slept on the ground, flagellated himself and secretly underwent many other mortifications of the flesh in order to purify himself. His virtue was so great that Pope Clement VII named him Canon of Notre Dame de Paris, then Bishop of Metz in 1384, then Cardinal. Pierre de Luxembourg strongly supported Pope Clement VII throughout the Great Schism, and the Pope called him to Avignon as a counselor on 23 September 1386. However, he died soon after, on 2 July 1387, and was buried, at his request, in the paupers' cemetery. He was chosen as patron of Avignon in 1432 and beatified in 1527. Some relics of his body lie in Saint Didier church, and his hat, his stole and dalmatic can be seen at Saint Pierre church.

The patron saints of Avignon

Sainte Marthe

Saint Martha came from an illustrious Israeli family. She gave everything she had to help the poor. Because she was a disciple of Christ, she was persecuted by the Jews and set adrift in a rudderless boat with her brothers Lazarus and Maximin, her sister Marie-Madeleine, and Marie-Jacobée, Marie-Salomé, Trophime and Sarah. However, angels saved the drifting boat and guided it to Provence, to land in a place since called "Saintes-Maries-de-la-Mer".

Lazarus went to Marseille and became the city's first Bishop. Trophime became the Bishop of Arles and Maximin founded the archdiocese of Aix-en-Provence. Marie-Madeleine became a hermit, in Sainte-Baume. Martha went to Avignon to convert the people living along the Rhone river, in particular in the city of Tarascon, where she battled the Tarasque monster for which Tarascon is possibly named. She was at the head of a community of women. At her death, her body was buried by Christ, and many pilgrimages were made to her tomb.

The **Tarasque** or Drac is a mythical beast in the Rhone. It had the head of a lion, with teeth as sharp as swords. The body was covered with scales and a spiked shell, with a row of needles sticking out. It had a long coiled tail and six sharply-clawed feet. The Tarasque could live under water or on land. When in the woods, it killed everything in its path. Under water, it overturned all the boats. Saint Martha set out to find the monster and discovered it in the midst of devouring a man. She sprinkled holy water over it and made the sign of the cross. The Tarasque immediately became as meek as a lamb and Martha was able to put a leash on it. However, the people slaughtered it with stones and spears.

Saint Ruf

Saint Ruf is said to be the son of Simon of Cyrene. Historians say that Ruf actually existed. He was a priest and perhaps the founder or one of the first leaders of the Christian community in Avignon, in the 4th century. The Abbey which bears his name, built outside of the ramparts, was also a burial grounds and Ruf's body is said to be buried there. The Order of Saint Ruf, founded in 1309, was famous in the Middle Ages, and spread throughout all of France, Catalonia and northern Italy.

Saint Agricol

Saint Agricol was born in Avignon in 627, and succeeded his father, Saint Magne, as Bishop of Avignon. His great zeal stimulated an enthusiastic following, creating the need for new churches in the city. In the year 690, Agricol donated his own home for the construction of the Saint Agricol Church, which can be seen today. He is also said to be the founder of Saint Geniès, Saint Symphorien, Saint Pierre and Saint Didier churches. Through his prayers, Agricol saved the city from a long drought. However, the heavy rain which then fell caused an invasion of snakes. Agricol implored the heavens once again, and God sent storks to eat the snakes, and the sun came out. This explains why Saint Agricol is always shown accompanied by a stork, which is his "attribute", and why people pray to Saint Agricol when there is bad weather.

BÉNEZET'S EARTHLY REMAINS

Although Bénezet laid the first stone of the bridge, he did not live to see the bridge completed, for he died around 1184-1185. In an act dated January 1186, which set the regulations for the tolls to cross the bridge, his death is mentioned in these terms: "brother Benoît whom we remember as a very pious person". Saint Bénezet was so widely venerated that the Bishop and the canons wanted to have him buried in the Notre-Dame-des-Doms Cathedral. But Bénezet had chosen his own place of burial, which was to be above one of the piles of the bridge. A chapel was built to house his tomb, and it quickly became a favorite destination for pilgrims, as popular, it was said, as Notre-Dame du Puy-en-Velay. The chapel was full of crutches left behind by the lame and the crippled who were healed there !

But much later, in the 17th century, the bridge was in a poor state of repair and was in danger of collapsing. It was extremely risky to reach the chapel. The faithful were afraid to go there, to such an extent that in 1673, on Bénezet's feast day, no religious services were even held ! Moreover, Bénezet's remains could very well be carried off in the waters of the Rhone, if there were a flood !

The Archbishop of Avignon was moved by this state of affairs, and organized the **translation** of Bénezet's remains. On 16 March 1670, he had the tomb opened. The body was brought to the chapel in the hospital on the bridge, where it was displayed in a glass case.

However, these events set off a veritable conflict. All the parishes argued over who would get Bénezet's **relics**: Saint Agricol and Saint Madeleine churches, the Célestin Fathers and even the King of France, Louis the XIV, who claimed them by virtue of his **sovereignty over the Rhone riverbed** and wanted Bénezet to lie in peace at the Saint André Abbey in Villeneuve !

The Celestin Couvent

To restore calm and order, the body was laid back in its original tomb on the 3rd of May 1672, and a compromise was sought and finally reached. It was decided that Bénezet would lie in the **Celestins Convent**, which was located in Avignon but which was a royal establishment. On the 26th of March 1674, an immense crowd attended the magnificent ceremony. Many years later, in 1690, the Celestin Fathers had the Chapel of the Duke of Orléans renovated by the Avignon architect Jean Péru in order to house the tomb of the saint, which was placed there on the 9th of February 1693. When the French Revolution occurred, there was talk of transforming the convent into a library and a museum. In 1791, Meynet, the **constitutional priest** of Saint Didier church, decided to safeguard Bénezet's relics by sheltering them in Saint Didier. He opened the tomb and discovered the body dressed in an **alb** and a **dalmatic**. One ear was missing, stolen in 1670 by a surgeon who had removed it for his own keepsake ! The limbs were held in place with brass wires. Unfortunately however, transferring the relics to Saint Didier did not provide the hoped-for safety, for the church was later turned into a prison. Some of the prisoners opened Bénezet's **reliquary** and dragged the body throughout the church. However, during the night, some of the other prisoners saved what they could of the body, which they gave to their families to hide. Only the head remained in the church. It was hidden in a gilt box which was not discovered until the 19th century.

Saint-Didier

22

On the 12th of July 1790, the Civil Constitution of the clergy was voted into law. All priests had to take an oath of loyalty to this Constitution if they wanted to continue to perform their duties, which, from then on, were to be paid for by the national government. This law had a lasting negative effect on the relations between the Catholic church and the revolutionaries, and caused a split between the refractory, or "non-juring" priests, and the constitutional, or "juror" priests. **Vincent Meynet** (1739-1804) canon of Saint Agricol church, took the oath before the town authorities of Avignon and was appointed **juror priest** at Saint Didier in 1792. In 1795, he became the curator of the Avignon literary deposit and Museum.

the Bienheureux Pierre de Luxembourg Chapel

The Célestins couvent was founded on the site of a small cemetery reserved for paupers who claimed to be ruled by Papal law (as opposed to municipal Avignon law). Out of humility, Pierre de Luxembourg requested to be buried there. Several miracles occurred on his tomb. The Queen of Sicily, Marie de Blois, had a wooden chapel erected there. Pope Clement VII then founded a monastery there, which he bestowed upon the Celestin monks. However, the King of France, Charles VI, declared that he was the founder. His uncles, the Duke of Berry and the Duke of Burgundy, and his brother, the Duke of Orleans, laid the first stone in his name on the 25th of June 1395. In the 15th century, a monumental chapel was erected to honor Pierre de Luxembourg. The chapel was later redecorated in the Baroque style during the 17th century. The square adjacent to the Celestin convent is called "Corps Saint" (Holy Body) square, due to the nearby tomb of Pierre de Luxembourg. When Bénezet's relics were transferred to the Celestin convent, the name was changed to a plural, and since that time the square has been known as "Corps Saints", or Holy Bodies !

The decision was made to gather the various scattered relics and place them at the Grand Seminary in Avignon, which was done as well as possible. Then, on the 1st of January 1854, the Archbishop of Avignon, Monsignor Debelay, transferred them to Saint Didier church, where they remain to this day, along with the relics of Pierre de Luxembourg. Thirty-two men carried the precious reliquary, under a canopy, all the way to the church. Clergy, soldiers and civil authorities accompanied the cortege. The streets were draped with banners and decorations, as the procession made its way toward the Corps-Saints square, bedecked for the occasion with flags and oriflammes. Ships' flags, specially brought in from Marseille, snapped in the wind, and images of the saints venerated in Avignon were hoisted throughout the city. An altar was prepared in the street. The city decided that Saint Bénezet would henceforth be celebrated for three entire days every year, in early July, at Saint Didier church. His statue would be carried in a solemn procession and the Archbishop would light a bonfire on Corps Saints square. At Saint Didier, a chapel was dedicated to the saint, and his statue remains there to this day.

The **alb** (from the Latin *alba*: white) is the white linen vestment that the priest wears over the cassock to celebrate Mass.

The **dalmatic** is a vestment which originally came from Dalmatia, and which was worn in Rome by deacons and bishops as of the 4th century. A dalmatic is a tunic with two vertical bands, and wide sleeves which end at the elbow.

A saint's **relics** can be the remains of the body, or just bones, or clothing, or objects which belonged to the saint, and which, due to the fact that he or she had touched them or been in contact with them, retain something of the saint's sacredness. The Church accepts the worship of relics. The **translation** of relics is the ceremony during which they are transported to a place of worship.

Bénezet's relics

St. Bénezet's relics which still remain at Saint Didier church are the head, the right foot, one vertebra, and some fragments of the skin. In the Cathedral, there is the right forearm, part of one hand, the upper half of the right thigh, one vertebra, one rib and one finger.

In 1980, the relics were examined by S. Gagnière, then curator of the Palace of the Popes. He drew the following conclusions: the bodily remains which had been gathered presented the same aspect and thus belonged to the same person. The man was of a slender build, but quite strong. He was approximately 1.65 meters tall. He was between 25 and 30 years old when he died. These facts certainly agree with the biographical data which we have from the past.

The **reliquary** (French: **châsse** comes from the Latin *capsa*: case) is a chest in which a saint's relics are kept. It is often quite ornate, sometimes decorated with precious stones and materials. In the Middle Ages, the construction of a chapel was linked to the presence of a saint's relics, thus the chapel served as an architectural envelope around the reliquary, before which pilgrims would kneel in prayer.

After the town of Avignon capitulated to Louis VIII's troupes in 1226, the king had the bridge destroyed, from the Villeneuve side of the Rhone all the way to Bénezet's chapel - that was the portion that the king considered his property. In the 14th century, discussions started back up between the papacy and the kings of France over who owned the entire Rhone riverbed. The interminable **trial of the Rhone** got underway and was only resolved four centuries later, after the French Revolution, when Avignon and the Comtat Venaissin became part of France.

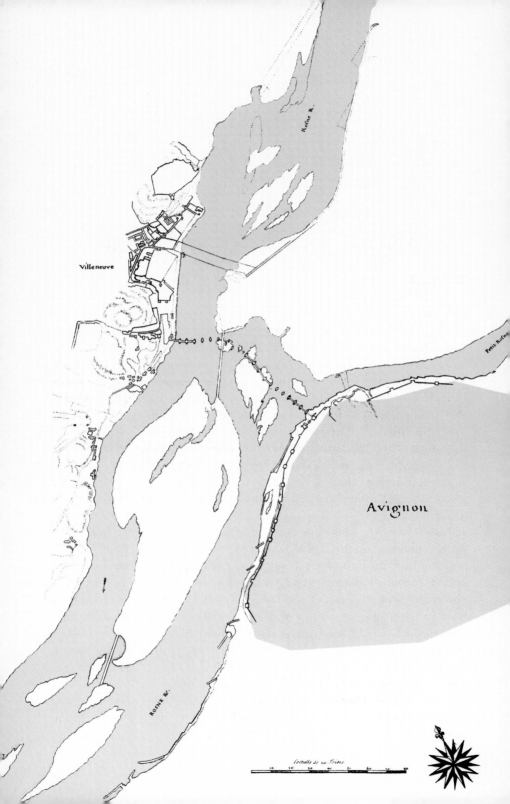

Villeneuve

Rosne R.

Petit Rosne

Avignon

Rosne R.

Eschelle de 10 Toises

ABOUT THE RHONE RIVER

TOPOGRAPHY

The Saint Bénezet bridge was built over a mighty and temperamental river, the Rhone. The city of Avignon was founded and grew in the sharp bend formed by the Rhone as it flows south. Avignon lies at an altitude of only 5 meters above the lowest water level. At Bénezet's time, the main stream of the Rhone was on the Villeneuve side of the river. This is where the harbor was located, just downstream of the Philip-the-Fair Tower. The hills which line the river, in Villeneuve and Bellevue, drive the water back toward the left bank, the Avignon side, which is lower in altitude than the right bank, except for the Rocher des Doms rock. The arm of the Rhone which flows alongside Avignon was quite shallow, barely navigable at low water, sprinkled with gravel and bars and sand bars which formed *iscles*, or little islands, and stands of willow. Where the Barthelasse Island stands today, there were several small islands which came and went depending on the floods and water levels. The name "Barthelasse" appeared for the first time in 1495, and the island connected with Piot Island, forming one single land mass, in the 19th century. Up until then, you could navigate between the two in a boat. The waters of the Rhone used to cover the lower areas of the city, to the west, and floods were a common, and catastrophic, occurrence in the history of the city. In the 19th century, a dam was built upstream, channeling the waters towards Avignon, which reversed the situation described above. The Villeneuve arm of the river no longer received harbor traffic and became instead a haven for fishing boats and the site of a few water wheels. Then, in the 20th century, work by the National Rhone Company once again re-channeled the water, and the deeper, more powerful arm of the Rhone flowed anew on the Villeneuve side.

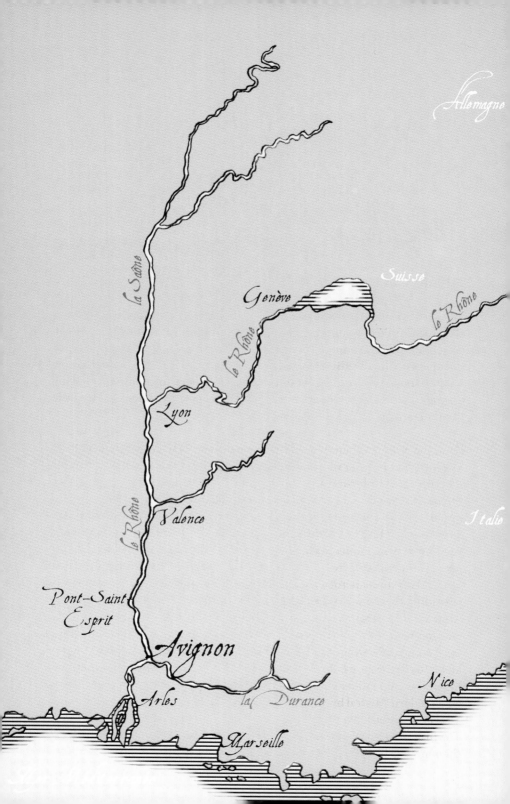

Allemagne

Suisse

Genève

la Saône

le Rhône

le Rhône

Lyon

le Rhône

Valence

Italie

Pont-Saint-
Esprit

Avignon

Arles

la Durance

Nice

Marseille

THE RHÔNE

The Rhone river is 812 kilometers long. It starts as a trickle on the slopes of Saint Gothard mountain, and switches southward, traveling through oft-changing landscapes. It is the only channel which links north-west Europe with the Mediterranean coast at such a low altitude. There are many tributaries, and the Rhone valley is subject to flooding. Flowing through marshy wetlands at the end of its journey, the Rhone ends at the Mediterranean Sea.

Of all the rivers in France, the Rhone is the most powerful and the swiftest. The riverbed is quite wide in spots. Its form and level change frequently, creating great obstacles to navigation. Yet, the Rhone has been an important axis of communication since prehistoric times. The Phoenicians sailed the Rhone, transporting amber and tin from north to south. Traveling up the Rhone river, the Greeks entered Gaul and left behind a very strong influence. The Rhone was the major artery for Roman expansion, and was frequently traveled to supply Rome with goods from Gaul. Many Roman roads started from the Rhone river banks in Lyon, spreading throughout Gaul. Large sailing ships, sea craft and slave galleys from the high seas could sail up the Rhone all the way to Arles, where people and goods would be transferred to river boats. In terms of business, there were companies which traded with the Far East, as well as with the Rhine and Moselle regions. River trade relied on a shipping fleet which was organized into guilds called *nautes*, a colorful and lively group of people who Frédéric Mistral brought back to life in his work "Le Poème du Rhône". This commercial river trade was also the route that Christianity traveled. The invasions and divisions which took place in the kingdoms of the Franks then made the Rhone a border between France and the Germanic Empire.

Hauling was how goods were brought upriver. The boats, chained together one behind the other, were pulled by 12 to 30 horses, depending on the size of the string of boats. It took approximately thirty days to go from Arles to Lyon. Going downriver was faster of course, but more dangerous. **Water coaches** were used - these were wide, flat-bottomed boats with a big rudder, which transported both persons and goods up until the late 19th century. From the Mediterranean to Arles, **lighters** or hoppers were used. These were light, flat-bottomed boats with a lateen sail and a triangular jib, which were well-suited to coastal trade and river shipping.

Castles and strongholds sprang up along the river. The right bank of the Rhone was designated as the "Kingdom", the left bank - the Avignon side - was designated as the "Empire". Regions slowly formed around Lyon , the capital of Gaul, and an important European center.

The waterway was bordered by a road which lined the left bank. Starting in the city of Vienne, a second road traveled further inland, going through the towns of Romans, Crest, Grignan, Saint-Paul-les-Trois-Châteaux, Vacqueyras and Carpentras. However, almost all heavy transportation went by the river.

During the Middle Ages, goods traveled to Lyon on wooden rafts which themselves were then sold as firewood upon arrival. **Shipments hauled** by sheer manpower, then by horses, traveled upstream, against the current. The towns of Lyon, Beaucaire and Arles grew and developed into very active river ports.

Heavy barges, called *caupuli, taverniers* (48-tonners), and long boats, called *sardines* (24-tonners) traveled up the Rhone to transport salt from Fos, and stopped to pay the **tonlieu** just below the Rocher des Doms. In the year 1192, boat traffic was intense, and barges increased in size to 64-tonners. Wood from the regions around Die and Valence was floated down the river on 30-meter by 7-meter rafts, steered and punted by the crew. These rafts were also used to ship other kinds of goods. Wheat, which was an increasingly widespread crop thanks to the many grinding mills in Avignon, was transported to Genoa via St. Gilles. In the late 12th century, new types of goods were circulating: wool for the weavers, the resources needed by the dyers (ferns, chalk, cochineal), tin, copper, iron and lead, hemp and pine-pitch, fleece and leather. Rope-making and leather-working were two very prosperous local industries. The fabric

trade led to steady relations between Marseille and Naples. Foodstuffs also traveled, such as root vegetables, fava beans, figs, chestnuts, bacon, oxen and heifers which were butchered at the slaughterhouses, ewes, lambs, fish, eels, table salt and preserving salt, pepper, ginger, cumin, wine and oil .....

In Avignon, there was great hustle and bustle all along the banks of the Rhone. To the southwest, there was the "Périers" or stone-cutters' port, where all manner of building materials were unloaded. The main port was just by the bridge, opposite the "Eyguière" entrance (today called "porte du Rhone"). Upstream, at the Aurose entrance (today called the "Porte de la Ligne") was the port for wood, where the entrance was marked by an old archway, since disappeared, called the Portalet. Another port was built at the Saint Lazare entrance. Jetties were built to keep the fast current far from the banks.

This very lovely drawing, part of which remains simply sketched by pencil, is a rare upstream view of the entire length of the four remaining arches, prior to the restoration work. The walls of St. Nicolas chapel are in good condition, but the chapel was no longer used. Against the pier, in front of the Châtelet, you see the profile of the chapel built in 1715 by the Bargemen's Brotherhood, to replace St. Nicolas chapel. The dock is busy, with goods being unloaded and registered at the Port Bureau, located on the first bridge pier. There are carts, and a coach. On the other side of the river, some boats are being hauled upstream by horses and men. The condition of the Poulin Tower, and the absence of the building which replaced the Salt Storehouse in 1815, date this drawing from before the Restoration.

Alain Breton

EXPLORING THE BRIDGE

Together, let's take a look at what remains today of this very complex construction. As you walk through the streets in the La Balance neighborhood, you come to the exit from the Popes' Palace underground parking. The **ramparts** which protected Avignon during Bénezet's day stood farther into the city than the 14th century ramparts which stand today, for the city was smaller. The first circle of ramparts connected to the rock just about where you are standing now. Most probably, the bridge also came up to this point. Archeologists have hypothesized that there was one more arch, and thus another bridge piling, which would have been located just where you are standing.

On your right, regally perched on the hill, stands the Archbishops' Palace, today the Petit-Palais Museum. Behind you, crooked rue Ferruce runs to the Porte du Rhone. In the bend made by this street, stood the **Saint Bénezet hospital and the hospital chapel**.

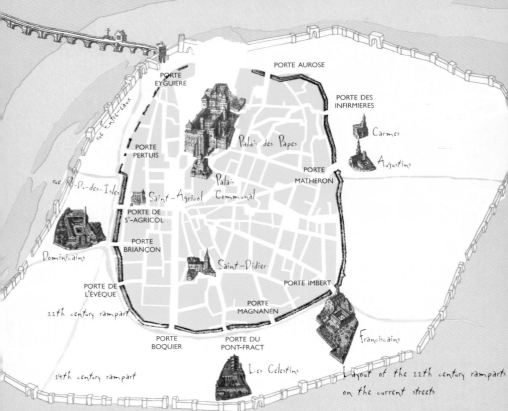

Layout of the 11th century ramparts on the current streets

The 11th century ramparts

In the 2nd century, Avignon was a Roman city, and was quite possibly surrounded by ramparts, since several vestiges of walls have been discovered during past road work. Also, several accounts describe the walls during the Low Empire, a time when the city had shrunk back around the base of the rock to protect itself from barbarian invasions, occupying only one-fourth of its previous area. In the 11th century, a new rampart was built, along the lines of the original Roman rampart. It was roughly rectangular in shape, ran approximately 3000 meters, and enclosed approximately 45 hectares. There were twelve entrances into the ramparts, and the Porte Eyguière, which means water, was near the bridge. Now Joseph Vernet street runs where these 11th century ramparts once stood. One arm of the Rhone ran in what is now Limas street (Limas means silt deposit). The river also flowed along the Grande Fusterie area, in the lower part of what is now Annanelle street, near Joseph Vernet street, and ended at the Saint Roch gate into the ramparts. Between this arm of the river and the main stream, there were gravel beds, which formed little islands, called *iscles* . The Dominican convent was built on one of these little islands. There were other islands in what is now the Champfleury area and the Courtine area, which in the 19th century was still referred to as Courtine Island. In the 18th century, there was a street named "Entre-Eaux" or Between-the-Waters, which today is the Rempart-du-Rhône street (see the map from 1836), and a street called "Notre-Dame-des-Isles", or Our Lady of the Islands, now called "rue du Mail", or Mail street. The 11th century ramparts were lined with a second wall in the 13th century, with trenches between the two, filled by water from underground rivers and two canals, one from the Sorgue river and the other from the Durance river. Although the King of France had ordered the total destruction of the ramparts during the 1226 siege, they were not completely razed. However, they were dismantled bit by bit after 1251, when the Commune bowed to Charles of Anjou and Alphonse de Poitiers.

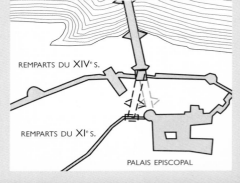

REMPARTS DU XIV\e S.

REMPARTS DU XI\e S.

PALAIS EPISCOPAL

Audouin Aubert

Etienne Aubert, who became Pope Innocent VI, occupied a cardinal's residence located on the site of today's City Hall. After Etienne Aubert became pope, his palace went to his nephew, the cardinal Audouin Aubert, who undertook significant renovation work. He ordered the construction of a large tower, in which the city installed a clock in 1471. This became the Clock Tower which today dominates "Place de l'Horloge", or Clock Square, and after which the square was named. Inside the tower, a bracket sculpted in the form of a cardinal is said to be Audouin Aubert's portrait.

THE BRIDGE HOSPITAL AND THE HOSPITAL CHAPEL

In the Middle Ages, when a bridge was built, a hospice was most often built along with the bridge, as a work of charity, to provide aid and assistance to traveling pilgrims. The hospice was a place to stay the night, when the rampart entrances were locked. Sick and poor travelers could also take shelter there. In 1181, the Bridge Works purchased land to build a hospital at the entrance to the bridge, near the buildings where the lay brothers shared a dormitory and a refectory. In 1370, the hospital they built became part of a nearby hospital, which had been built seven years before by the nephew of Pope Innocent VI, **Audouin Aubert**. At that point, it could treat approximately sixty patients. Then, it was destroyed in 1398, during a siege against the Palace of the Popes. The community of the Bridge Works brothers had died out, but the hospital continued to admit the sick and the poor. The hospital building had a ground floor, which was often flooded, and one upper floor.

On the drawing from 1618, you can see the hospital building and its chapel, adjacent to a high square tower crowned with machicolations. This is the **Poulin** tower, which jutted out from the ramparts downstream from the bridge. Today its original shape can no longer be recognized.

To the south-west of the hospital, a small courtyard contained the cemetery, just next to the houses on rue Eyguière. Only the lay brothers or foreigners could be buried in this cemetery, so as not to compete with the parish cemeteries in the city. To the north-east, which would be your right, a courtyard was bordered by the access ramp which led to the bridge. The surface was very solidly paved in order to survive the Rhone's raging flood waters, and the ramp was surrounded by walls.

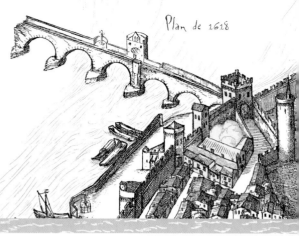

Plan de 1618

Jean-Baptiste Péru was born in 1676. He was the oldest son of architect Jean Péru, and took over his practice upon Jean Péru's death in 1723. Jean-Baptiste Péru never attained the reputation of his contemporary Jean-Baptiste Franque. In addition to his work around the bridge, Péru designed plans for the stairway and plaza for the Notre Dom des Doms cathedral, but his death in 1744 kept him for completing this project which then went to his competitor, Franque.

Observe the façade which runs the length of the street. As you can see, there is nothing medieval about it, for the area was renovated and the original appearance of the buildings has totally vanished. The access ramp to the bridge was destroyed in 1729. The modern wall encloses a larger space and a new access to the châtelet was opened. You can see it right in front of you. The new opening is the majestic, Doric style entrance designed by architect **Jean-Baptiste 1 Péru.**

To the left is the **entrance to the hospital chapel**, which the Brothers had obtained permission to build in 1187. The hospital later became the seat of the "**Confrérie des Portefaix**", the **Brotherhood of the Dock Hands** of the Rhone, or "Gagne-Deniers", a group which was founded in the late 16th century. As we have already seen, the body of Saint Bénezet was transferred here from 12 May 1670 to 3 May 1672, following the collapse of two of the arches of the bridge. In 1713, the architect **Pierre Mignard** enlarged the hospital. Then **Jean-Baptiste Franque**, another renowned architect, rebuilt the damaged façade in 1744.

A large portico made up of two engaged pillars holds a triangular pediment which runs the width of the building and is embellished with a frieze of rosettes at the bottom. In a scroll inset, the following words were inscribed:

D.O.M.
DIVO BENEDICTO PONTIS
SACRUM MDCCXLV
(To the greatest God,
to Saint Bénezet of the bridge, in the year of Grace 1745)

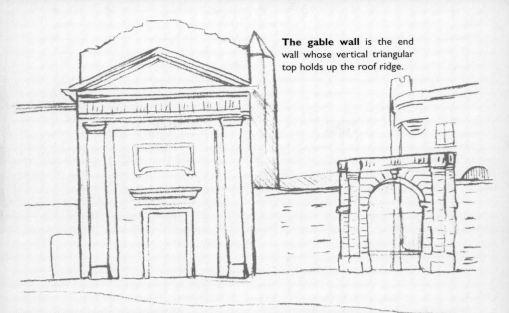

The gable wall is the end wall whose vertical triangular top holds up the roof ridge.

The hospital through the ages

In the Middle Ages, hospitals were not as big and important as modern-day hospitals are. In Bénezet's era, Avignon had twelve different hospitals. However, even the biggest ones had only a few dozen beds. The Brothers of the Bridge Works lived as a community under the authority of a prior. With the money they collected, they financed the maintenance of the bridge and covered all the costs of the bridge hospital. The bursar brother purchased the food and the hosts for communion, and sewed shrouds for the dead. When the popes lived in Avignon, the fabric was supplied by the Pontifical almonery. One brother looked after the vineyards and the barnyard. Another begged for the oils needed to treat the sick. A sister was in charge of laundry, other sisters cooked and cared for the sick. There was a paid nurse in charge of medical care, who did not belong to the community of the Bridge Works. However, as of 1278, the prior had embezzled all the income, the faithful no longer gave so enthusiastically, and the Bridge Works' finances were in ruin. So the city of Avignon took over administration of the bridge and turned it over to two **rectors** who ran the hospital and paid wages to the surgeons and the nurses. The lay brothers no longer did anything but minor tasks. Once again, to revive the interest of the faithful and stimulate new gifts of money, the legend of Saint Bénezet was spread throughout the region and indulgences were granted.

In 1370, the hospital joined forces with Audouin Aubert's hospital, which was more modern. The last of the lay brothers died, and the community ceased to exist in the 15th century.

A nurse ran the hospital on the meager income which remained after the maintenance of the bridge was paid for. The people who were sheltered in the hospital were no longer fed, but had to beg for their meals. The hospital celebrated its feast day on Corpus Christi day. The hospital feast day continued to be very successful, for we see that in 1476, 312 letters of absolution were sold to the faithful.

However, by the 1600's, the condition of the bridge had seriously deteriorated, and the hospital was only very sporadically used. Its activities were reduced to burying drowning victims in the cemetery which ran along the north wall of the chapel, and providing wine, bread and a bed to pilgrims traveling through. Then, in 1678, there was a revival of hospital activity, to treat the victims of scrofula. The hospital was given all the goods from the Saint Lazare leprosy, which had closed for lack of patients, and it thus grew from a capacity of twelve beds to thirty in 1750. Doctors from the city of Avignon treated the hospital patients. At the end of the century, the dilapidated condition of the bridge, and the fact that Bénezet's relics had been transferred to the Celestins convent could have meant the end of the Bridge Works. But because the young people afflicted with scrofula had to be isolated from other patients, they were sent to the bridge hospital, which was maintained to treat approximately twelve adolescents. With the French Revolution came the end of the bridge hospital. Its belongings were sold off, and all activity was transferred to Saint Martha Hospital. The bridge hospital was definitively closed in 1807, and the building was put up for sale in 1839.

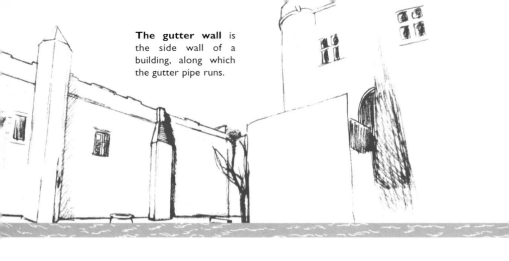

The gutter wall is the side wall of a building, along which the gutter pipe runs.

You can still see the inset where these words were once sculpted. The scroll inset was demolished to make room for a window, which has since been filled in.

On your left is Ferruce street. Jean-Baptiste Franque designed the arches which spring from the ground floor, where shops were set up in the past. Two doors, topped by a cornice, led into upper-class homes which the hospital intended to transform into sickrooms. These homes had lovely large rectangular window on the upper floor. The cemetery disappeared during this new work.

Now, let's turn around and go through the monumental door. The city rampart forms the back of the courtyard, between the Poulin Tower, against which the hospital leans, and the little fort, or "châtelet" which defends the access to the bridge. On the left, you can see the chapel building. In this building, there was an office, the sickroom with sixteen beds, the kitchen where the housekeeper slept, and an attic. A turret in which there is a spiral stairway, and the hood of the fireplace, jut out on the "**mur gouttereau**", or wall with the gutter.

The transformations which took place during the 18th century made the courtyard more spacious. The common room was enlarged and a new kitchen was built in a new building against the rampart, creating a connection between the Poulin Tower and the châtelet. On the ground, you can still see the bases of the walls of this building, parallel to the rampart. It was most certainly also at this time that a salt storehouse was

The Book of the Dock Workers' Statutes

also built against this part of the rampart wall, on the outside. A garden and a cobblestone barnyard were also added. In the courtyard, there were two wells which can still be seen, one in the northern corner, the other at the foot of the châtelet.

Looking up, you can see the entrance to the châtelet, and you can see for yourself the slope of the ramp which once led to it. Architect Jean-Baptiste Péru replaced the ramp by a stairway, which meant that horses and carts could no longer use the bridge. The stairway no longer exists, and nowadays, you must climb up scaffolding stairs. Above the entrance, Avignon's coat of arms can still be seen, and two mullion windows still light up the second story.

Poulin Tower, named after its 19th century owner Mr. Poulin, was divided up into apartments in the 19th century. Today it is not as high as it originally was, and windows have been created. There remains a single mullion window, which was discovered when an adjoining building was demolished.

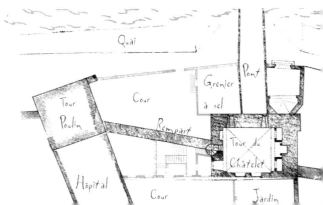

The Brotherhood of the Dock Hands, or the "gagne-deniers"

This Brotherhood was founded in 1596, and took Saint Bénezet as its patron saint. Members of the brotherhood vowed to help each other, and shared the task of unloading the boats that it owned with another, older brotherhood, the Brotherhood of Notre Dame de la Paix, whose seat was at the Notre Dame de la Principale church. Members of the Brotherhood of the Dock Hands always carried a canvas sack slung over their shoulder, which they needed for their work. The term "gagne-deniers", which means "penny-earners" appeared in 1622 and indicated that they earned a mere pittance. The number of dock hands, a turbulent and even dangerous group, later the real hotbed of the French Revolution in Avignon, swelled with the invention of steamships.

Jean-Baptiste Franque was born in Villeneuve-les-Avignon on 1 February 1683. Son of a master mason, he too became a mason and settled in Avignon. He became an architect around 1715. His talent and his excellent reputation earned him many faithful clients. Two of his ten children, François and Jean-Pierre, also became architects and assisted him. They worked throughout the south of France, from Toulon to Carcassonne and north to Viviers. François finished his career as a member of the prestigious Royal Academy of Architecture. Jean-Baptiste Franque strongly influenced artistic life in Avignon, and left an immense body of work. Among other works, today we can admire Saint Charles chapel, the butcher shops and fish markets on Vieux-Sextier street, part of the Alms House, the Caumont House and the Villeneuve-Martignan House. He died in March 1758.

THE CHATELET, OR SMALL CASTLE

When it was built, Saint Bénezet hospital was at the very head of the bridge, and the old châtelet must have been located, as we have seen, near the entrance to what is now the underground parking lot.

In the 14th century, the Papacy settled in Avignon (see another book in this collection: *Avignon, un Palais pour le Prince de l'Eglise*). According to historians, Avignon's population jumped from 5,000 people to 30,000. New neighborhoods were built outside of the 11th century ramparts, and a new rampart was needed to enclose these areas. In 1355, a 4330-meter long wall was built. This wall connected with the bridge at the first arch.

In 1366, Pope Urbain V, who ruled from 1362 to 1370, began the construction of a fortified entrance tower, known as the châtelet, into the ramparts. At first the King of France, Charles V, was strongly against this idea, but later accepted it. Then, in 1375, during the papacy of Pope Gregory XI (1370-1378), this tower was demolished and a bigger fortified entrance was built. Most of the work was done by 1382. The main entrance was embellished with a gilded statue of Saint Peter done by Barthélémi Cavalier (who also sculpted the tomb of Pope Innocent VI). The roof of the entrance, covered with sheets of lead, was topped with a bell-tower, whose bell was blessed by Cardinal d'Aigrefeuille on the 27th of June 1378. There was also a brass ball with a cross on top. This tower was crenelated, and had small corbel turrets on either side. However, during the **Catalan War**, which raged from April 1410 to 23 November 1411, the Avignon troupes destroyed the tower, on the 12th of September 1410. The Catalan troupes, who were defending Pope Benedict XIII, fled from the tower, abandoning their munitions and supplies.

41

In the 18th century, the hospital was granted authorization to install the Rectors' office in the Châtelet. A stairway replaced the former entrance ramp. Jean-Baptiste Franque covered the room with a vaulted ceiling in 1734. Painted shields, bearing the coats of arms of the Avignon consuls and vice-legates decorated the walls. However, these vanished in 1984.

Only one fragment still remains, and you can see it as you enter, on the left wall. You see a helmet which is part of a knight's coat of arms.

In April of 1411, a temporary tower was built of dry stone, without any mortar. When the city was able to afford it, they built a new tower, most certainly re-using the foundations dating from Pope Gregory XI's time. The first stone was laid on the 15th of June 1414.

This tower entrance through the ramparts forms a rectangular mass, with the widest side along the axis of the bridge. There are two stories, built over a cellar level. It faces the Philip the Fair Tower on the Villeneuve side of the river, which we will discuss a little later on. Entering the ramparts, you go through a wide, pointed doorway, and enter a large room which leads to the bridge. There is a second door with a portcullis which was controlled from the upper floor. This upper floor was built in 1489-90 by Antoine Carteron, a native of the Bourges diocese. The spiral staircase in the southern turret, on your left, was extended to lead to the new second story. Crenelation, loophole windows, and four corbelled watch-turrets were then added to the tower. Since then, it has not been modified, except for the machicolations, which were destroyed in the 18th century.

As you cross over the drawbridge, lift your gaze and you will see the traces of the coats of arms which decorated the river side of the Châtelet, just below the windows which open on to the portcullis room. You can see the arms of the city of Avignon, those of Pope Innocent VIII (1484-1492) and those of the Archbishop-Legate of Avignon (1476-1503) Giuliano Della Rovere, future Pope Jules II.

However, before going any farther, go back into the main room and take the small stairway to the north which leads out onto the old watchman's path on top of the ramparts. From this walkway, you can see the entire bridge.

Avignon

Innocent VIII   Julien de la Rovère

the Rector's office

The Catalan war

Pope Gregory XI, who ruled from 1370 to 1378, had returned to Rome to attempt to re-establish the papacy there. When he died in Rome, the Great Western Schism broke out, dividing the Christian world in two. Seven successive Italian popes were elected. In counter-elections, two other popes were also elected, and returned to Avignon. These were Pope Clement VII (1378-1394) and Pope Benedict XIII (1394-1409). After winning a first siege at the Palace of the Popes in 1389, Pope Benedict XIII fled in 1403 and was deposed in 1409 by the Council of Pisa. The Papal states were defended by his nephew Rodrigue de Luna. However, in 1410, Avignon and the Comtat Venaissin followed France's lead in joining the ranks behind the Italian Pope, John XXIII. The Palace of the Popes was once again attacked. This battle was called the Catalan War, after Rodrigue de Luna's Catalonian origins. Rodrigue de Luna held the Palace, the Rocher des Doms, the cathedral and the Petit Palais, around which a defensive wall had been built, and the Châtelet on the bridge. Rodrigue resisted for seventeen months, before surrendering on the 2nd of November 1411, when he relinquished the Palace of the Popes to François de Conzié, Chamberlain to Pope John XXIII.

43

The Roman Boat Bridge in Arles

THE BRIDGE

Bridges had been built in the past to cross the turbulent Rhone river. The most famous are the Pont Saint-Bénezet d'Avignon and the bridge in Saint-Saturnin-du-Port, which became the town of **Pont-Saint-Esprit**. Whether made of wood, of stone or even of boats lashed together, these bridges were quite remarkable for each one meant a hard-won victory over the rough waters, and often did not survive for long. For centuries, **trail ferries** had been used. These were ferries with two rudders, one at the prow, one at the stern, which were guided by a cable on a wire which stretched from one bank to the other over the river.

Building a bridge over the Rhone was an extraordinary feat at the time. After the destruction of the bridge in Arles, and prior to the construction of the Pont Saint Esprit, the Pont d'Avignon was the only bridge between Lyon and the sea. It provided a passage to the merchants and pilgrims who were traveling to and from Italy via the Alpine passes. It channeled the traffic from the Via Domitia that had previously used the Arles bridge. The bridge built in Avignon brought increased trade and traffic to the city, making Avignon a more important and more cosmopolitan city. However, construction of the bridge also ruined the ferry trade, which had been a significant source of profit to the Bishop (who received one-third of the money paid for crossing the Rhone), and for the Amic family, and for some knights who also partook in the profits. The Bridge Works negotiated with the harbor masters and the families who owned the rights to the ferry traffic. The Works granted them part of the tolls that were paid to cross the river. Then, as of 1187, the Works bought the rights to the **carrying tax.** Back then, much like on today's toll roads, fees were paid to cross the bridge. A pedestrian paid one *obole*, a horse and rider paid two

When there was no bridge across the river, which was most often the case, boats ferried men and goods, in exchange for a **carrying tax**, which was paid to the Bishop and the chapter, and to aristocratic families, such as the Amic family, who descended from the Viscounts of Avignon.

Pont-Saint-Esprit

The legend of the bridge in the town of Pont Saint Esprit is similar to the legend surrounding Saint Bénezet. There too, a young shepherd met an angel who showed him where to build a bridge, a chapel and a hospital. Like Christ and his Apostles, the number of bridge builders came to only thirteen ! One of them, quite a mysterious character, was so zealous in his work that he accomplished much more than all the others. He was always the first on the site in the morning, and yet disappeared in the evening without demanding his pay. The local population decided that it was the Holy Spirit, disguised as a simple laborer, who had thus helped build the bridge. This explains the name of the town, Pont Saint Esprit, named by the community of the Bridge Works after the Holy Spirit.

Lyon Pont-Saint-Esprit Avignon Arles

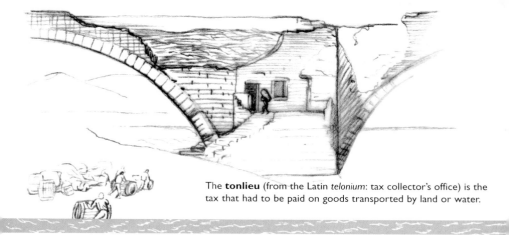

The **tonlieu** (from the Latin *telonium*: tax collector's office) is the tax that had to be paid on goods transported by land or water.

deniers, a horse and cart paid four, a donkey one, and one *obole* per head in flocks of sheep and herds of pigs. Once the bridge was built, the number of crossings doubled. The community of the Bridge Works purchased land, gardens and vineyards in and around Avignon, and bought a **parish church** in Rognonas in 1213, building up their possessions to earn income to pay for the bridge. These resources enabled them to do maintenance work on the bridge, for it required constant, costly upkeep due to the frequent, violent flood waters, which uprooted trees and hurled them against the bridge piers. Every time the bridge was impaired, the city lost part of its income. In addition to the tolls that were paid, taxes were also levied on the unloading of goods. The river port in Avignon brought in 40,000 *sous*, which was approximately one-third of the amount made in the sea port of Marseille.

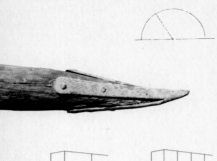

A round arch is a full semi-circle. The exterior curve of the visible face of the arch is called the extrados, the inner curve of the arch is called the intrados.

Carbon 14 testing: All living organisms contain a constant level of carbon 14, a naturally radioactive isotope. Dead organisms lose half their content of carbon 14 after 5730 years. After 11460 years, they have only one-fourth the original amount. By measuring the carbon 14 content of the organism being studied, it is possible to date it fairly accurately.

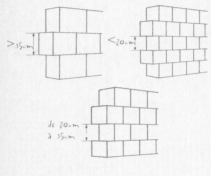

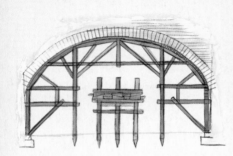

"Appareillage" or the fitting of stones, means the way that stones are cut and assembled together in a construction. "Grand appareil" or masonry in large courses, is an assembly of large stones, laid in layers of the same height, often without the use of a binding mortar. The stones are sometimes bound together by iron clamps. "Moyen appareil", or middle course masonry, uses smaller stones and often makes up the outside facing of thick walls. "Petit appareil" uses small rubble stones, often square, submerged in cement.

The "tablier" or deck of a bridge means the platform which is held up by the bridge piers and over which people travel.

Saint Bénezet's bridge's wooden deck
Between each bridge pier, rows of stakes driven into the river bed held up the planks of the deck. These stakes filled in the space between two bridge piers. Five of these stakes have been brought to the surface. Two of them had iron clamps on them to avoid splitting the wood when it was driven into the river bed. Three of the stakes were made of oak and were over 3 meters long and 0.44 meters in diameter.

The construction technique
On the bank, the form-work for the stone was prepared on top of a wooden base. This base was then positioned in the river and lashed into place, as well as possible, given the strong river current. The masonry foundations were then built on top of this base, which acted like a pontoon. When it was fully loaded with the foundations, it would sink, and the base remained in the river bed, stuck under the weight of the stone masonry foundations, where it acted as a bed plate.

In 1965, during work on the riverbed, the Compagnie Nationale du Rhône discovered thick wooden planks under the four remaining pilings of the bridge. These planks were between 20 cm and 1.10 meters thick. The wood was tested by the **carbon 14** method, and was dated somewhere between the year 290 and the year 530 AD. Counting from the Avignon side, the bridge pilings were under the thirteenth to the seventeenth arches, and they were in very poor condition. These pilings were also studied and photographed in 1969. They were made of pine beams which were dated from the 9th and the 13th centuries.

A BRIDGE BEFORE THE BRIDGE ?

It has been suggested that during the Roman era, there was already a bridge across the Rhone at Avignon. If such a bridge existed, it is presumed that it was built in stone, was approximately 5 meters higher than Saint Bénezet's bridge, and had **round arches** built in large course masonry. It is presumed that the bridge was destroyed at an unknown date.

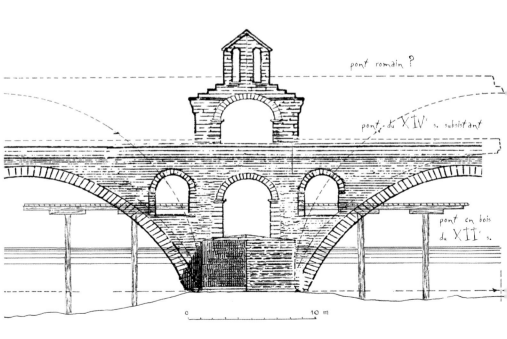

ao este mebiat ecert eamaruit
adesaurem lacorta queuconoscloz ardit
ala pmeuu corta podem estre suffint
oltra sira louttransa si eli so descofit
bzant leuas la coira olobzuit eleserit
li couu elas twuipas elf graslef esclarzit
n tota la ribeura elo eap esbaudit

eli puublo ensemble cau taut euant
dmf la maoz prcissa leson entreferit
al ploz de bel cauc foron le acuillit
al ubram de colomba elacer rebullnit
las maillas redoudas eli elauel bullnit
laraclas moluas eli escut forbit
li dart elas flechas eli cauel polit
peuas esagretas eli espicut brandit
ig caualers abloz uales eamaruit
is siruens elsalgrcs queuo tozardit
las autras prurlas debc ferir auzit

The Albigensian Crusade was led against heretics who refused the truths as taught by the Church. The Cathare (from the Greek catharos: pure), or Albigensian heresy (so-called because it spread around the region of Albi), advocated a religion based on austerity, which clashed with the moral laxity of the Church. The Cathares were protected by the Count of Toulouse, Raimond VI. After the Pope's legate, Pierre de Castelnau, was assassinated in January 1208, Pope Innocent III (1198-1216) raised a crusade against the Cathares, which turned into a massacre. The barons from the north of France took advantage of the situation to take over the Languedoc area. They confiscated the areas of Béziers and Carcassonne and entrusted their administration to Simon IV, Count of Montfort. Simon de Montfort became extremely powerful. In 1212, he defeated Raimond IV in the Battle of Castelnaudary, and in 1213 won the Battle of Muret, against Raimond's ally King Peter II of Aragon, who perished in the battle. In 121 5, he seized Narbonne and Toulouse. Also in 1215, at the Council of Latran, the Church dispossessed Raimond VI of his county, which was given to Simon de Montfort. But the Provençal people rebelled, forcing Simon de Montfort to do battle in the Rhone valley, and Count Raimond was able to recover his land. In 1221, a second crusade was launched, where King Louis VIII (1223-1226) fought in person and besieged Avignon. The Treaty of Paris, in 1229 gave the land conquered by the Montforts to the Kingdom of France. The Comtat Venaissin was given to France in 1271, then Philip III the Bold (1245-1285) gave it to Pope Gregory X in 1274. The King remained the co-lord of Avignon up until 1291 when King Philip the Fair gave Avignon to the Count of Provence Charles II of Anjou.

THE BRIDGE BUILT IN THE MIDDLE AGES BY BÉNEZET

By the Middle Ages, the deck of the Roman bridge had long since been destroyed, if indeed there had ever been a bridge in Roman times. All that would have been left would be the stones from the bridge pilings, and Bénezet and his companions could have re-used these Roman pilings in building the "**tablier**" or wooden deck of their bridge. This is one hypothesis, which gains credibility from a very important document which refers to "the wooden bridge that Avignon had built". This document was the letter that the French barons sent to Emperor Frederick II, suzerain of the city, to justify the siege of Avignon. Work on Bénezet's bridge lasted seven years. However, other historians think that there never was a Roman bridge. Their assumption is that all the materials that dated from before the Middle Ages were just old materials that had been re-used by the bridge builders in Bénezet's time.

Bénezet's bridge had twenty-two arches which spanned 915 meters. As we have already seen, there could have been a twenty-third arch. This hypothesis is supported by the discovery of the vestiges of a bridge piling in 1982, near the current châtelet.
In 1184, at Bénezet's death, a chapel was built on the second bridge pile. The floor of the chapel would correspond to the height of the bridge deck in the Middle Ages. In 1226, the King of France, Louis VIII, accompanied by one of the Pope's **legates**, the Cardinal de Saint-Ange, and a large troupe of soldiers, launched a new **Crusade against the Albigeois**.

A **legate** (from the Latin legatus: envoy, delegate) is an ambassador.

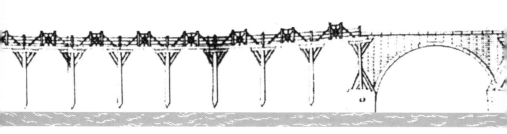

The Commune of Avignon, at the height of its power at the time, sided with its suzerain, Count Raymond VI of Toulouse, and refused to let the King pass through the city on his way to Albi. The King laid siege to Avignon, and after three months of blockading the city, from the 10th of June to the 12th of September, Avignon, brought to its knees by famine, surrendered. The King's revenge was brutal. In addition to paying a ransom and delivering hostages, Avignon had to destroy the ramparts, demolish three hundred "**maisons fortes**", or fortified houses, and three-fourths of the bridge.

We do not know when the bridge was rebuilt. It was most probably fairly rapidly rebuilt, for in 1237, Pope Gregory IX rebuked Avignon for having started repairing the bridge in spite of the royal ban. In 1275, a person named Alfant du Marchéneuf donated the sum of ten pounds to finance the construction of one stone arch after his death. The arches often broke, either due to the violent river waters, or because royal agents destroyed them, claiming possession of the Rhone and of the bridge. When an arch was broken, ferries came back into use, or a temporary framework enabled people to cross.

A "**maison forte**" or strong house is a dwelling which is fortified with defensive elements such as towers, walls, crenelation ...

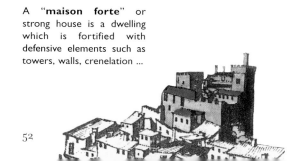

THE BRIDGE AT THE TIME OF THE POPES

In the 14th century, the Popes, who had settled in Avignon, turned their attention to maintaining their valuable passage over the Rhone. In 1317, Pope John XXII (1316-1334), hired stone cutters Jean Foucaud and Pierre Audibert to work on restoring the bridge. In 1343, Pope Clement VI (1342-1352), allocated a goodly sum of money to restore four stone arches. This work took many years, and was supervised by Cardinals Bertrand du Pouget and Annibal Ceccano, and performed by Pierre Foucaud, called Capelier and his brother Bertrand.

New work was reported in 1360. In 1375, two carpenters repaired wooden arches under the supervision of Cardinals d'Albano and d'Ostie. In 1380, Pope Clement VII financed the fortification of the wooden part, and the construction of four stone arches to support it. In 1411, during the Great Schism, the Catalonians who supported Pope Benedict XIII set fire to one of the wooden arches and cut away one of the stone arches, in order to protect the Châtelet. A carpenter rebuilt these arches in 1418. In 1453, the Cardinal of Foix, the Pope's legate, gave the Montfavet Priory to the community of the Bridge Works, in order to provide them with sizable revenues earmarked for bridge repair and maintenance.

A second chapel was built above the chapel where Saint Bénezet's tomb lay. The floor level of the new chapel corresponded to the new deck. This new chapel was dedicated to Saint Nicolas, patron saint of bargemen, and was consecrated in 1411. An apse was added in 1513.

WHAT WE CAN SEE TODAY

Today, there remain only four arches of the bridge. These arches are 42 meters wide and confer a gracious lightness to the bridge. These arches are **three-centered arches**, or depressed arches, a design which allowed for separating the bridge piers, to let the strong current flow, without making the bridge too high. This technique, which is quite spectacular, was also used in Pont-Saint-Esprit.

Later, as you walk along the road under the bridge, you will see that the first arch is made of four juxtaposed arches. You can see this same type of construction on the lower level at the Pont du Gard. This technique is not easy, but it does save on wood for the **template** and keeps the masonry from collapsing in the event of a sharp thrusting movement, since each arch is independent. In Avignon, the first arch is the only arch which strictly applied this construction technique.

The rectangular bridge piers have triangular breakwaters both upstream and downstream, which served to deflect the current. The stones to build these breakwaters most probably came from the Amelier quarry, located in Villeneuve, at the base of the Fort Saint André. This quarry was long referred to as the "Pont d'Avignon quarry". Stone from the Mas de Carles, to the north of Villeneuve, was used for the higher parts of the bridge, more visible and carefully built, and for Saint Bénezet's chapel. This stone was also used to build the Palace of the Popes.

Two ecus decorate the first arch. Perhaps one of them commemorates the gift of 200 florins donated by Hugues de Sade in 1355. This decoration was apparently reproduced in 1418, when the arch was rebuilt. The second ecu contains interlaced initials SL, whose meaning is not known.

In the 17th century, the docks along the Rhone river were developed. **Statues of the patrons saints of the city of Avignon** were erected there. The statue of Saint Agricol, sculpted by Jean-André Borde, went up in 1629, just opposite the Rhone gate entrance in the ramparts. A fresco by Philippe Mathieu shows the old port on the Rhone with the colossal statue. This painting is hung in Saint Agricol Church, but is hidden by the organ. The statue of Saint François was upstream of the bridge, and a little farther, there was a statue of Our Lady. In 1674, Jean Péru sculpted a Saint Bénezet just opposite the Oulle gate entrance into the ramparts.

In the 19th century, the boatmen's group added a **mariner's cross** on top of the first arch, near Saint Nicholas chapel, the seat of their brotherhood. A statue of Saint François was erected just in front of the breakwater on the first bridge pier. The statue survived the great flood of 1674, though just the head remained above water. This event gave rise to the popular saying: *When Saint François drinks, Avignon will sink.* During the flood of 1747 a fisherman's boat was moored to the statue, and caught the statue which was torn off the breakwater by the flood waters. The statue was re-erected once again, then vanished for good in 1792. The second bridge pier holds up the two chapels built one on top of the other. Some very old engravings show that there was a type of wall on the downstream side. This construction is difficult to date, and could be from the era that the châtelet was built, or from the 16th century. It could also have been built to go with the fortified apse which was added in 1513. The last vestiges of this wall disappeared during the 19th century, when some very poor restoration work was undertaken. The third bridge pier, called "the Cross pier" after the cross it supported, was rebuilt between 1575 and 1578. This pier bore a column which was topped with a capital on top of which there was a cross.

The mariners' cross
Many boats have their "chapel" at the stern. This was a cross, in wood, sometimes up to 1.50 meters high, which was fastened to the helm, or on the wheel. All the different symbols and instruments related to the Passion hung from the cross.

As you cross over the drawbridge, you may notice that the deck of the bridge slants slightly, approximately 1 cm per meter. The first arch is in the axis of the châtelet. Then, the bridge veers 60 cm toward the downstream side between the first and third arch. After the fourth arch, however, it veers 1 meter 60 on the upstream side ! The slanted deck and the zigzag layout are due to the fact that these four arches were built to connect the châtelet, which was built in 1348, to part of the bridge which was older. The bridge angled sharply upstream at the fifteenth arch to reduce the impact of the current . Today, the deck of the bridge is protected by a wrought iron railing. In the past, a parapet had been erected on the upstream side to protect travelers from the violent winds.

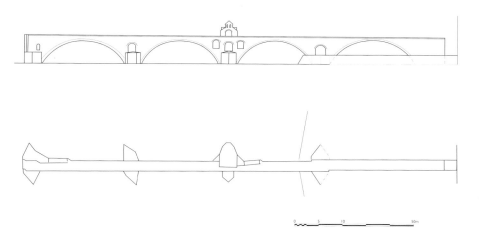

SAINT BÉNEZET CHAPEL

The lower chapel is the sole remaining vestige from Bénezet's era.
This small oratory was built to shelter his tomb. It was also a place where
the pilgrims, who were among the many visitors traveling over the bridge,
could come and pray. The lower chapel was built at the same time as the
bridge pier upon which it rests. The chapel's level therefore most
probably corresponds to the height of the bridge deck in the 12th century,
which is 4.50 meters lower. However, since then it has undergone so
many modifications that it is difficult to imagine what it looked like at the
outset. The chapel occupies the rectangular part of the bridge pier.
Its apse is on the breakwater, and the nave juts out 3.60 meters upstream.
You entered the chapel from the west, through an open porch, then a
semi-circular arched doorway. Now, a staircase has been carved out of
the thickness of the arch. The **gable wall** was topped with a triangular
pediment.The embedded half-columns were topped with **Corinthian
capitals**, which can be seen in the corners. They most probably bore an
architrave. Two **arch bands**, which come down on to the Corinthian
capitals, form the edge of the nave. The semi-circular **apse** had a **semi-
domed** vaulted ceiling. The side walls were reinforced with a double
offset arcade. A **strand of ovum**, originally part of the Saint Bénezet
chapel and today still visible in the upper chapel, ran along the edge of the
barrel-vault. To the south, a window is embellished with roses and long
sculpted branches.

When the bridge was re-built in the 13th century, this western door was sealed off, and you entered the chapel through an inside stairway. This may be why a new door was later opened on the south wall, slightly overlapping the original southern window. The height of the nave was altered, and covered with diagonal ribs which came down somewhat inelegantly on to four small columns. The upper chapel became the bargemen's chapel, and was dedicated to their patron saint, Saint Nicolas.

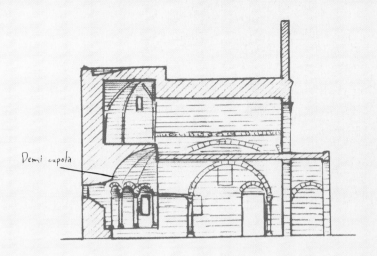

Demi cupola

The nave (from the Latin navis: ship) is the middle and side aisles of a church from the entrance to the crossing chancel, where the faithful gather. **The choir** (from the Latin chorus: song) is the part of a church between the sanctuary and the nave, reserved for the singers and the clergy. **The apse** is the part of the church behind the altar.

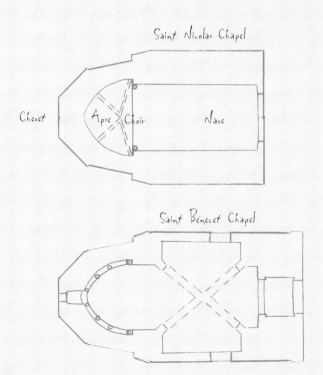

Saint Nicolas Chapel

Chevet   Apse Choir   Nave

Saint Bénezet Chapel

SAINT NICOLAS CHAPEL

This chapel was built in the late 14th century at the same level as the new height of the bridge deck. Like the lower chapel, it was damaged during the **Catalan War**. The apse was re-built in 1513. It extends beyond the roof of the Romanesque nave, which makes it look like a tower. It has a sexpartite vault ceiling, and is lit by a small rectangular window on the eastern side. The **nave** opens to the west, through an arched doorway. On the outside wall, traces of two slopes and the base of vaulting leave room to think that a porch was re-built at one point. The roof was and still is covered with **roofing stones** and was crowned with a small double-arched bell-tower from the 16th century.

Starting in 1715, the clergy from Saint Agricol church refused to hold liturgical services in Saint Nicolas chapel, for they found the access to be too dangerous. The **Brotherhood of the Bargemen** replaced it with a small building below the bridge, against the abutment-pier of the bridge. If you face the châtelet, you will see it on your left, on the same level as the road. This chapel now lies in ruins, however the ruins can inspire your imagination to see how it once looked. The façade had a semi-circular arched entrance way and a round window, with a bell-tower on top. The chapel was badly damaged during the 1856 flood. During the 20th century, it was converted into housing for the guardian of the bridge.

From the deck of the bridge, you can drink in the beautiful view all around. You can see the Philip-the-Fair Tower. This tower was originally the other end of the bridge, yet you can clearly see that it is far from a straight line between where you are and the tower where the bridge ended !

Saint Nicolas originated from Patras and was the Bishop of Myre. Sailors caught in a storm implored Saint Nicolas for help. He heard their prayers, helped them handle their boat and calmed the waves. The sailors went to Saint Nicolas church and gave thanks, recognizing the saint without ever having seen him before. But the saint attributed his miracle to divine mercy and to the faith of the sailors. Another story about Saint Nicolas tells about a nobleman who prayed to Saint Nicolas to have a son, and promised a gold cup for the church in exchange. His prayers were answered, and he ordered the cup, which he then liked so much that he kept it for himself and substituted another of equal value. The father and the son brought their offering by sea. The father told the son to dip the cup into the sea for some water, and the child fell and drowned. The sorrowing father went to the church, but as soon as he placed the cup on the altar, the cup fell to the ground. Upon this, the child reappeared, safe and sound, the cup in his hands. He told the amazed onlookers how Saint Nicolas saved him from the sea. This is why Saint Nicolas is the patron saint of sailors and river men.

PHILIP THE FAIR TOWER

At the time of the Commune, Avignon ruled over the Saint Andrew abbey and surrounding houses on the other side of the Rhone. However, after Avignon capitulated to King Louis VIII following the siege of 1226, the king concluded a feudal treaty with the village, which was later confirmed by Philip the Fair in 1292. The king raised the village which had grown around the abbey to the status of a *"ville neuve"*, or new town. He made the new town part of his kingdom, and granted financial incentives to anyone who chose to settle there. This treaty also guaranteed that the town would be protected, and provided for the construction of a fortress in the port, where the bridge ended. Today, all that remains is the tower which was built in 1303, by master builder Radulphe de Mornel. The tower has a trapezoidal layout, with a ground floor and one upper floor, constructed with projecting, rough-finished stone. A few gargoyles remain at what was originally the top of the tower. In 1307, a fortified entrance connected the bridge to the tower. The original plans for the fortifications called for larger buildings, but they were modified for diplomatic reasons. For the Count of Provence, Charles II of Anjou, and the Avignon people deemed that they had control over the right bank of the Rhone and were against such fortifications. On the 4th of October 1307, Avignon notables went to the tower, measured it, and threw a stone at it three times, declaring "I denounce this new construction". This conflict came to a halt when Pope Clement V settled in Avignon in 1309. The tower was raised to a height of 27 meters in 1360. On the smooth wall of the new floor, the corbelled latrines jut outwards. A watchtower projects 7 meters upward on the north side. The tower is crenelated on the top, with machicolations on all except the western side, where there is a parapet. There are look-out posts in all four corners. Inside, the three levels have vaulted ceilings on intersecting ribs, which end in beautifully sculpted brackets.

The bargemen or **"ribeyriers"** transported goods by boat whenever the bridge could not be crossed due to a fallen arch or other flood-related damage. The bargemen were very active in the 17th century, when the bridge was finally abandoned. They benefited from a monopoly in Avignon, which the king ended in the 18th century when he ordered that their activity be opened to the Villeneuve bargemen also. Their brotherhood was founded in Saint Nicolas chapel.

THE RUIN OF THE BRIDGE AND MODERN RESTORATION WORK

In 1582, wide openings were created in the tympanum of the bridge piers, which weakened them and accelerated wear. The bridge was definitively closed around 1650. In the late 17th century, three arches near the Isle of Argenton were damaged. On the island, four arches remained standing. However, over an arm of the river which ran between Argenton and the Isle of the Chartreux, there was a big gap where four arches were missing. A drawing from 1721 shows two arches on the Barthelasse Island, and a single arch adjoining the tower in Villeneuve. At the time, people took a ferry, which they boarded near the Oulle gate, to the Isle of the Chartreux. There, there was a road, largely built on pilings, which led to one stone arch. Here, one traveled across a bridge on wooden pilings, then on four stone arches, ending at the Philip the Fair Tower in Villeneuve.

Restoration of the four remaining arches on the Avignon side was begun in the 19th century. These arches were badly damaged and threatened to collapse at any time. A. Caristie, E. Viollet-Le-Duc and H. Révoil, architects from the Historical Monuments, and other architects from the *Ponts-et-Chaussées* and the *Compagnie Nationale du Rhône* all worked on this challenging task, which, most unfortunately, disfigured the bridge. For the main concern here was neither historical accuracy nor aesthetic considerations, but simply consolidation of a very weak structure.

To simplify the task, all the sloping parts of the bridge were leveled to a single horizontal plane, a window was opened in the second bridge pier, and the cross on the third bridge pier disappeared. The access to the châtelet was sealed over, and a stairway was built above the bargemen's chapel, which became the bridge guardian's house. Another significant change was that the cold stone used in this restoration work was very different from the molasse, or sandstone, which was originally used.

Now that you are more familiar with the bridge, let's take a stroll along the banks of the Rhone, and walk under the bridge arch which spans the road. The Rhone is an impressive river, and it both contributed a great deal to Avignon's prosperity and caused a great deal of misfortune, as you shall see.

THE FLOODS

The rising waters of the turbulent Rhone river were a veritable plague to the city. One common occurrence was that after the very dry spring and summer seasons, rain would fall in the autumn. The temperatures dropped, and the rain turned into snow at higher altitudes. Southern winds then blew, rain fell harder, and the early snow melted, swelling the many tributaries feeding into the Rhone. The Rhone river rose, but the Durance river, into which the Rhone flowed, would block the Rhone, keeping it from draining further downstream. A catastrophe was inevitable if a tributary's waters swelled at the same time, such as the Ardèche river, which could rise several meters in just a few hours. The sailors had a saying, printed here in the Provençal language: *"Se la Durènço coto e que vengue lou cop d'Ardecho, sian touti foutu"*, which meant: "If the Durance rises and the Ardèche does too, then we are doomed".

One very memorable flood occurred on 17 September 1226, just five days after Avignon had surrendered to Louis VIII's soldiers. Had this flood occurred just a little bit earlier, it may well have changed the fate of the city. As it was, it simply added to the inhabitants' great misfortune.

We know of nine floods during the 14th century: in 1342, in 1346 when the crops were destroyed, in 1352, in 1353 during the May Cross Festivities, when several pilgrims were drowned, in 1358, when the Saint Lazare entrance was destroyed and part of the ramparts swept away, in 1362, when the ramparts were destroyed between the Saint Michel entrance and the Limbert gate, in 1376, which shook the foundations of the Cordeliers Church, and in 1398.

Of the 15th century floods, the 1433 catastrophe has remained quite famous, for the miracle of the Separation of the Waters took place. On the 29th of November, the Rhone, the Durance and the Sorgue rivers

all overflowed their banks and filled the low-lying areas of Avignon. The Church of the Gray Penitents was quickly filling with water, and the members of the Gray Penitents brotherhood feared that the Blessed Sacrament would be swept away. They decided to carry it to safety and hurried to the chapel by boat. Entering the church, they saw for themselves that the waters had separated, flowing around the altar and the choir, leaving them totally dry and intact. On the 1st of December, crowds of people came to see that the furnishings on the altar and in the choir were not even damp !

In the 1471 flood, two arches of the bridge were swept away and a section of the ramparts near the Limas area was destroyed.

The 16th century had its share of cataclysms, including the 1544 flood where 400 meters of the city walls collapsed, and cadavers floated out of the graveyards at the Carmes church and at the Augustinian church ! The citizens of Avignon fled to the high slopes of the Doms Rock. In 1548, the *porte de la Ligne* disintegrated, and the waters gushed above the pendentive which held up Saint Bénezet chapel.

The biggest flood in the 17th century occurred in 1674, when most of Avignon was under water for several days.

The 1755 catastrophe was long held to be the worst ever, for there was flood after flood for over two months, in October and November. On the 29th of November, several batardeaus, or movable dams, gave way, and surging water overwhelmed the city, reaching a height of 7.23 meters !

However, this calamity was unfortunately surpassed in 1840, with flood heights reaching over 8 meters. On the 2nd of November, flood victims hacked holes in the roofs of their homes to escape from the rising waters. The water reached the lower chapel on the bridge, and the thirteenth

step of the stairway to Saint Agricol church. Measures were finally taken to halt the damage inflicted by the capricious waters, with the construction of dikes, valves, sewers, and earthen counter-walls built up against the ramparts.

In 1856, a flash flood overwhelmed the city on the 31st of May, with 4.11 meters of water in 45 hours time. A valve gave out between the Saint Dominique and Saint Roch entrances into the ramparts, sweeping away 30 meters of the city walls. A 1.50-meter high wave surged into the city, flooding nearly the entire city and wreaking total havoc. Emperor Napoleon III arrived on the 3rd of June, visiting the devastated city from a boat to judge the extent of the damage. A boat dock had been temporarily installed on the plaza in front of Saint Agricol church. The emperor went to the Doms Rock, and to City Hall, where he gave Mayor Paul Pamard a check for 50,000 francs.

There was more heavy flooding in November and December 1935, when water levels reached 6.95 meters.

Since 1946, the construction of dikes and dams has theoretically meant the end of flooding in Avignon. However, there continues to be great damage to the homes and crops on the Barthelasse Island, and floods remain a source of great concern.

AFTER THE BRIDGE, OTHER BRIDGES

Ever since the end of the 17th century, Saint Bénezet bridge has been unusable, and all traffic crossing the Rhone was done by boat or ferry. It was not until the 19th century, when Guillaume Puy was mayor of Avignon, that new work on the bridge was undertaken, between 1806 and 1812, done by the engineer Duvivier. He built a wooden trestle bridge which measured 224.80 meters long, and was divided into 15 bays. This trestle bridge was built opposite the Porte de l'Oulle entrance into the ramparts. It crossed the left arm of the Rhone river and led to a 226-meter long deck which connected it to the wooden bridge over the Villeneuve arm of the Rhone, which was 438 meters long and spanned 30 bays. This combination made the entire bridge 889.28 meters long. In February 1812, the construction of the bridge was completed over the Avignon arm of the Rhone. However, it was only opened to vehicle traffic in 1817. Traffic over the two parts of the bridge was only allowed in early 1819, and was subject to a tax. On the 26th of September 1821, although the weather was perfectly fine, three of the bridge supports collapsed on the Avignon side. Further collapse occurred in 1830. The great flood of 1840 demonstrated that the bridge, as it was, could not hold

up over the navigable part of the river. A temporary platform was built parallel to the former bridge on the upstream side, to provide for passage during the new construction work.

A suspended bridge was opened to traffic on 22 October 1843. This bridge connected with the wooden bridge on the Villeneuve side up until 1910, when it was replaced with a stone bridge. It was partially destroyed in June 1944 during bombing by the British air forces, and was repaired after France was liberated.

In 1972, river traffic was once again channeled to the Villeneuve arm of the Rhone, and it was quickly realized that the arches of the bridge were too low to allow river boat passage. The bridge was demolished, and replaced by the bridge which stands today, the "Pont Daladier". With the advent of increased automobile traffic, a second bridge, the "Pont de l'Europe", opened in July 1975, providing increased access between the Gard and the Vaucluse.

Edouard Daladier was a government minister several times (Minister of War, Defense Minister, Foreign Affairs), then leader of the government in 1933 and 1934, 1938-40, and member of the National Assembly. He was elected mayor of Avignon from 1953 to 1958.

A SWEET SONG TO END ON

Now you have discovered the history and legends of Saint Bénezet bridge, you have learned about its architecture, its setting and the many events relating to its history. To complete your mastery of this subject, all you need to know is the history of the beloved song, "sur le pont d'Avignon...". There were already songs about the Pont d'Avignon way back in the 15th century, however we have lost all trace of these songs except for one, which was sung for weddings in Normandy. These wedding songs were called "pillow songs" for they were traditionally sung to the newlyweds as they entered their nuptial bedroom. One of these songs about the bridge, brought by French emigrants to Canada, still exists in Canada. As for the well-known children's round, "Sur le pont d'Avignon", it was originally composed in the 1800's by Adophe Adam, and was sung at the Opéra Comique in Paris on 2 February 1853, in a play called "The Deaf Man or the Full Inn", which was set in Avignon. Three years later, an operetta entitled "Sur le Pont d'Avignon", which also featured the popular song, enjoyed resounding success.

Since then, the song has made its way throughout the entire world, and has added to Avignon's fame and reputation more than any advertising could have ever done ! And no one can claim the credit for this other than Saint Bénezet, who continues to watch over Avignon's destiny...

ERIN & Cⁱᵉ, imp.-édit.

SUR
LE PONT
d'AVIGNON

* Ronde *

ALLEGRETTO

Sur le Pont d'A-vi-gnon L'on y dan-se, l'on y dan-se, Sur le Pont d'A-vi-gnon L'on y dan-se tout

Les beaux Mes-sieurs font comm' ça, Et puis en-cor comm' ça.

On continue en citant des no
de professions, et alors qu'on di
— font comm' ça
pour chacun, on imite leurs
gestes. On reprend ensuite le re

➤ REFRAIN ➤

Sur le Pont d'Avignon
L'on y danse, l'on y danse;
Sur le Pont d'Avignon
L'on y danse tout en rond.

Les Professeurs
Les Écoliers
Les Polissons   font
Les Demoiselles   comm'
Les belles Dames   ça.
Les beaux Messieurs
etc...

Les Militair's
Les Comédiens
Les Avocats   fo
Les Cordonniers   con
Les Valets d'chambre ç
Les Capucins
etc...

Photographic credits

A Brief Bibliography

BRETON (A.), GAGNIERE (S.), MOGNETTI (E.), PICHOU (H.): "Saint Bénezet", dossier published for the exhibition held at the Petit Palais Museum in Avignon (November 1984-February 1985), Mémoires de l'Académie de Vaucluse, 1984.
BRUGUIER-ROURE (L.): "Les constructeurs de ponts au Moyen Age, récits légendaires ou historiques", Bulletin Monumental, 1875.
BRUGUIER-ROURE (L.): "Saint Bénezet et les frères du pont", Bulletin du comité de l'art chrétien du diocèse de Nîmes, 1890.
GAGNIERE (S.): Notes historiques sur les inondations d'Avignon, Rullière Frères, 1936.
GAGNIERE (S.): GRANIER (J.), Images du Vieil Avignon, Rullière-Libeccio, 1972.
GIRARD (A.): L'aventure gothique entre Pont-Saint-Esprit et Avignon du XIIIe au XVe siècle, Edisud, 1996.
GIRARD (J.): Evocation du Vieil Avignon, Editions de Minuit, 1958.
MARIE (D.-M.): Le pont Saint-Bénezet, étude historique et archéologique d'un ouvrage en partie disparu, Histoire et réalités, Versailles, 1984.
MOULINAS (R.) (ouvrage collectif, sous la direction de): Histoire d'Avignon, Edisud, 1979.
PANSIER (P.): La Tour du pont d'Avignon, Annales d'Avignon et du Comtat Venaissin, 1930.
PANSIER (P.): "Les Chapelles du pont Saint-Bénezet", Annales d'Avignon et du Comtat Venaissin, 1930.
PANSIER (P.): "Les anciens hôpitaux d'Avignon", Annales d'Avignon et du Comtat, 1929.
PERROT (R.), GRANIER (J.), GAGNIERE (S.): "Contribution à l'étude du pont Saint-Bénezet, Mémoires de l'Académie de Vaucluse, 1971.
ROUQUETTE (J.-M.): Provence romane, Zodiaque, 1974.
THIRIOT (J.): Note topographique sur la tête du pont roman d'Avignon, Avignon au Moyen Age, IREBMA,
LE BLEVEC (D.): Une institution d'assistance en pays rhodanien: les frères pontifes, Cahiers de Fanjeaux n°13.

Special thanks to Alain BRETON

Graphic Design
Saluces, Avignon
Illustrations
© Olivier Martin
Translated by Mary Podevin

Editions RMG-Palais des Papes 84000 Avignon
+33 (0)4 90 27 50 00
e-mail : rmg@palais-des-papes.com
www.palais-des-papes.com

Printing completed in March 2000
On the printing presses at Imprimerie Laffont, in Avignon
Legal deposit 1st quarter 2000
ISBN 2-906647-36-5 © RMG 2000